THE COOKIE LADY'S GUIDE TO GETTING TECHNICAL TEAMS
ON TIME

Bill Godecker

THE COOKIE LADY'S GUIDE TO GETTING TECHNICAL TEAMS ON TIME

iUniverse books may be ordered through booksellers or by contacting:

iUniverse
1663 Liberty Drive
Bloomington, IN 47403
www.iuniverse.com
1-800-Authors (1-800-288-4677)

ISBN: 978-1-4917-7250-8 (sc)
ISBN: 978-1-4917-7251-5 (e)

Print information available on the last page.

iUniverse rev. date: 07/28/2015

Dedicated to the Cookie Lady, Joyce Godecker, of B/E Aerospace, Anaheim on her 65th Birthday

Configurator: Sandra Arambula

Edited by: Matt Godecker

Contributors: Tammy Reid, Tommy Morland Reid X

CONTENTS

RAMBLINGS

In September of 2002 I landed in a job at B/E Aerospace in Anaheim, CA as Director of Engineering. There are a few twist and turns in how that happened, but leave it to say; a blustery customer supply chain lady at Airbus may have used her considerable influence.

Having changed jobs previously, my wife, Joyce, had traditionally stayed behind for two or three months until things settled down. Then she would use her feminine whiles to track me down, no matter how far I had gone. This time however, perhaps fearing I might be improving at getting away she chose to take a leave of absence and came out at the same time.

I settled into B/E Aerospace as the Director of Engineering. The engineering team at that time was only about 25 people. My assessment was that they were all good people. The only thing lacking was decisive and cohesive management. Just someone who would say, "This way folks" and the caravan of cats would all turn in the same direction at once and off we'd go like the 7 dwarfs to the gold mine.

So after a few weeks I decided to call an all hands meeting. I prepared my best "we'll fight them on the beaches" speech and headed for the main conference room at 1:00 PM on Friday afternoon. I orchestrated my arrival for the stroke of 1:00 PM on the dot. I walked confidently through the open door and….well, there were only 3 other people there. Somewhat crestfallen, I started calling around trying to find people. I remember calling Vince in the lab, "Ah Bill, do we have to come, we're awfully busy". "Yes, Vince, you do".

I got several similar responses and I ended up cutting the meeting short. Did Churchill ever run into this?

When I got home, as was our nightly ritual, we were having a glass of wine before dinner and she asked me if I had had a bad day. Was it that obvious? So I explained what I was trying to do and that I had failed at the one thing I think I'm good at. "Did you have anything for the engineers to eat?" She asked. "Uh, No". I hesitated. I think she would call that a well, "duh, moment."

As the following payday Friday rolled around I asked her what she thought I should use for bait to the meeting. She said something about cookies. Then she thought a moment and said "Why don't I bake some fresh cookies for you, I've wanted to bake something for a while anyway".

So when the time approached engineers began to straggle in with that "do I have to" look. But as they began to jockey for the cookies, the ice broke, laughter and conversation broke out around the room. Like most people who think they are good leaders, I probably gave my version of "we have nothing to fear" speech. But it didn't matter, at that moment the cats, including me, were herded together as bests as engineers can be. And I had nothing to do with it!

The Payday Engineering Cookie Meeting became legendary over the years and not just at B/E Anaheim. More later, but now for some recipes.

1.0 FEMALE CHOCOLATE CHIP COOKIES

Ingredients

Amount	Item
2 ¼ Cups	Flour, all purpose (Gold Medal)
1 Tsp.	Baking Soda (Arm and Hammer)
1 Tsp.	Salt
1 Cup	Butter
¾ Cup	Granulated sugar
¾ Cup	Brown Sugar
1 Tsp.	Vanilla (McCormick's)
2	Large Eggs
2 Cups	Semi-Sweet Chocolate Chips (Nestle)

Directions

Number	Step
1	Combine Flour, Baking Soda and salt in a small bowl
2	Beat butter, sugars and vanilla in large bowl until the mixture is smooth
3	Add eggs and mix in thoroughly
4	Gradually mix in flour mixture
5	Stir in chocolate chips
6	Let sit for 15 minutes
7	Drop 12 rounded tablespoons on to a cookie
8	In a 350°F preheated oven bake for about 10 minutes or until golden brown
9	Remove from cookie sheet when done and place each on a clean kitchen table top, allow to cool for one hour

3

2.0 MALE CHOCOLATE CHIP COOKIES

Ingredients

Amount	Item
2 ¼ Cups	Flour, all purpose (Gold Medal)
1 Tsp.	Baking Soda (Arm and Hammer)
1 Tsp.	Salt
1 Cup	Butter
¾ Cup	Granulated sugar
¾ Cup	Brown Sugar
1 Tsp.	Vanilla (McCormick's)
2	Large Eggs
2 Cups	Semi-Sweet Chocolate Chips (Nestle)
1 Cup	Chopped Walnuts

Directions

Number	Step
1A	Follow directions from 1.0, but add the 1 cup walnuts with the chocolate chips
1B	Or, split 1.0 recipe in half into separate bowls, add ½ cup chopped walnuts to one of the bowls
2	Remember! Never cohabitate the male and female cookie mix or the cookies!
3	In a 350°F preheated oven bake for about 10 minutes or until golden brown
4	Remove from cookie sheet when done and place each on a clean kitchen table top, allow to cool for one hour

3.0 MALE AND FEMALE M & M COOKIES

Ingredients

Amount	Item
2 ¼ Cups	Flour, all purpose (Gold Medal)
1 Tsp.	Baking Soda (Armand Hammer)
½ Tsp.	Salt
¾ Cup	Butter
1-1/3 Cup	Brown Sugar
1 Tsp.	Vanilla (McCormick's)
2	Large Eggs
1+ Cups	Semi-Sweet Chocolate Chips (Nestle)
½+ Cup	Chopped Walnuts

Directions

Number	Step
1	Combine Flour, Baking Soda and salt in a small bowl
2	Beat butter, sugars and vanilla in large bowl until the mixture is smooth
3	Add eggs and mix in thoroughly
4	Gradually mix in flour mixture
5	Stir in chocolate chips
6	Let sit for 15 minutes
7	Drop 12 rounded tablespoons on to a cookie sheet
8	In a 350°F preheated oven bake for about 10 minutes or until golden brown
9	Remove from cookie sheet when done and place each on a clean kitchen table top, allow to cool for one hour
10	For Male version, see Steps 1-4 of Recipe 2.0

4.0 APRICOT NECTAR COOKIE

Ingredients

Amount	Item
2 ¾ Cups	Flour (Gold Medal)
1 Tsp.	Baking Soda (Armand Hammer)
¾ Cup	Granulated Sugar
¼ Cup	Packed Dark Brown Sugar
2 Sticks	Salted Butter (Melted)
1	Large Egg
¼ Cup	Apricot Nectar
½ Cup	Apricot Preserves
¾ Cup	Dried Apricots, Chopped

Directions

Number	Step
1	In a medium bowl, combine flour and baking soda
2	Mix well with wire whisk and set aside
3	In a large bowl blend sugars with an electric mixer at medium speed.
4	Add butter to form a grainy paste. Scrape down sides of bowl
5	Add egg, apricot nectar, and apricot preserves. Beat at medium speed until smooth
6	Add flour mixture and apricots, blend on low speed until just combined. Do not over mix
7	Drop by rounded tablespoons onto ungreased cookie sheets 1 ½ inches apart
8	Bake in 300°F preheated oven for 19 to 22 minutes, or until cookies just begin to brown at the edges
9	Remove from oven and let cookies cool on the cookie sheet 5 minutes,
10	With a spatula remove to the kitchen table

5.0 MALE WHITE CHOCOLATE CHIP/ BUTTERSCOTCH CHIP COOKIES

Ingredients

Amount	Item
2 ½ Cups	All Purpose Flour
1 Tsp.	Baking Soda
¼ Tsp.	Salt
2 Sticks	Unsalted Butter, softened
1 ½ Cups	Packed brown sugar
2	Large Eggs
1 Tbsp.	Light molasses
2 Tsp.	Vanilla Extract
2 Tsp.	Good Single Malt Scotch
1 Cup	Chop Pecans
¼ Cup	Butterscotch Chips and White Chocolate Chips

Directions

Number	Step
1	In a medium size bowl combine flour soda and salt
2	In a large mixing bowl combine butter and brown sugar
3	Mix in eggs, molasses, vanilla extract, and the scotch
4	Blend in the flour mixture to the large bowl
5	Stir in the pecans and butterscotch and white chocolate chips, do not over mix
6	Drop rounded teaspoons full on to a cookie sheet
7	Bake in preheated 300°F oven for 18 to 20 minutes
8	Remove from pan onto kitchen table

6.0 OATMEAL RAISIN CHEWS

Ingredients

Amount	Item
2 ¼ Cups	Flour
½ Tsp.	Baking Soda
¼ Tsp.	Salt
1 Cup	Oats (Quaker Oats, quick)
1 Cup	Pack Dark Brown Sugar
½ Cup	Granulated Sugar
2 Sticks	Salted Butter, Softened
2 Tbsps.	Honey
2 Tsps.	Vanilla Extract
2	Large Eggs
1 ½ Cups	Raisins

Directions

Number	Step
1	In a medium bowl, combine flour, soda, salt and oats. Mix well with wire whisk and set aside
2	In a large bowl, blend sugars with an electric mixer set at medium speed
3	Add butter and mix to form a grainy paste. Scrape down sides of then add honey, vanilla, and eggs.
4	Mix at medium speed until light and fluffy
5	Add the flour mixture, raisins, and walnuts and blend at low speed until just combined, don't over mix
6	Drop by round teaspoons onto greased cookie sheet, 1 ½ inches apart
7	Bake in a preheated oven at 300°F for 18 to 22 minutes or until golden brown
8	Immediately transfer cookies with a spatula to a flat kitchen table
9	For the female version don't add the nuts

7.0 AKONA CRANBERRY WHITE CHOCOLATE CHIP

Ingredients

Amount	Item
2 Cups	All Purpose Flour (Gold Medal)
½ Tsp.	Baking Soda (Arm and Hammer)
½ Tsp.	Salt
1 ½ Cup	Unsalted Butter, Melted and Cooled Slightly
1 Cup	Packed, Light Brown Sugar
½ Cup	Granulated Sugar
1	Large Egg
1 Cup	Dried Cranberries
1 Cup	Macadamia Nuts

Directions

Number	Step
1	Beat melted butter, brown sugar and granulated sugar until smooth
2	Sift and add flour, baking soda and salt. Mix until just combined.
3	Add chocolate chips, cranberries and macadamia
4	Roll dough into 2' balls and space them about 2 inches apart on a cookie sheet
5	Bake 15-20 minutes in a preheat 300°= oven until edges are set but center are still soft
6	Transfer cookies to kitchen table
7	For Wahine version leave out the nuts, the balls in number 4 cook flat anyway.

8.0 ORANGE CORNMEAL COOKIE

Ingredients

Amount	Item
1 Cup	Unsalted Butter, Softened
1 Cup	Sugar
1 Tsp.	Grated Orange Zest
½ Tsp.	Salt
1	Large Egg
2 Tsp.	Vanilla Extract
1 ½ Cups	All-Purpose Flour
1 Cup	Cornmeal

Directions

Number	Step
1	In a bowl, beat sugar, orange zest and salt until light and fluffy
2	Add egg yolk, beating well, then add the rest of the egg and vanilla
3	Mix until well incorporated
4	Sift flour and cornmeal and add to mixture. Mix until just incorporated
5	Divide dough in half, form into disks and wrap tightly in plastic wrap. Refrigerate until firm, at least 1 hour
6	Remove 1 disk of dough from refrigerator and cut in half. Return unused portion to refrigerator
7	Lightly dust counter with flour. Roll dough to ¼ inch thickness
8	Cut 2 inch shapes with a cookie cutter and place on cookie sheet ½ inch apart
9	Bake in 375°F Oven for 6 to 8 minutes or until cookies are evenly, golden brown. Transfer to kitchen table
10	Repeat with remaining dough

ABOUT TIME

The chronology of a cookie week for the Cookie Lady:

Sunday: *Check the Fridge and Cupboard for bulk items; butter, flour, sugar, etc. During normal shopping buy bulk items as required*

Monday: *Get cook book out and decide which cookies to make, buy additional condiments if needed*

Tuesday: *Morning with the "Golf Gals", afternoon; cookie prep time*

Wednesday: *Additional prep work, a batch or two complete if possible*

Thursday: *Bake cookies till you drop*

Friday: *Pack up cookies, send off to work with Bill, then… rest up*

Fact #1: *The Cookie Lady does not eat a single cookie during the process*

Fact #2: *I am not allowed to be around on Thursday morning of cookie week*

Fact #3: *I do not know what the cookies are until meeting time*

Fact #4: *Engineers are rarely on time for meetings*

Fact #5: *The Cookie Lady is an unusual woman about time: She will ask me the night before we're planning to go somewhere "what time will we leave in the morning"? I'll say "around 8:00 AM". At 10 minutes to 8:00 the next morning she will be pacing by the front door anxious to leave and tapping her toes waiting for me. Of course if I am the first one to the door and tapping toes, then we will leave precisely at 8:00. If she says to you "I'll meet you at 10:00, and she were to arrive precisely at 10:00, then she would consider herself 5 minutes late.*

Fact #6: *Engineers are rarely late for the cookie meeting and a high percentage are actually early.*

Jim Croce sang:

If I could save time in a bottle
The first thing that I'd like to do
Is to save every day 'til eternity passes away
Just to spend them with you

Ingredients

Amount	Item
9 Oz	Mixed Chocolate from bars; *like dark, bittersweet, semi-sweet and milk chocolate,*
¾ Cup	Heavy Cream
¼ Cup	Unsalted Butter
2 tbsps.	Instant Espresso Granules
2 Tbsps.	Bailey's Irish Cream
8 Oz	Mixed Chocolate from bars; *like dark, bittersweet, semi-sweet and milk chocolate,*
2 Tsps.	Vegetable Oil

Directions

Number	Step
1	Finey chop the first batch of chocolate bars
2	Place the chopped chocolate in a medium bowl.
3	In a heavy, medium saucepan, bring the cream and butter to a simmer
4	Pour the hot mixture over the chocolate in the bowls
5	Mix together the espresso granules and Irish Cream Liquor until dissolved
6	Let stand for 5 minutes then mix fill smooth
7	Cool to room temperature and then refrigerate for 2 hours
8	Roll the mixture into 1 inch diameter balls, place on a waxed paper lined cookie sheet, refrigerate after
9	In a double boiler melt the chocolate and then add the oil.
10	Using a fork, dip the balls into the chocolate until coated, return to cookie sheet and refrigerate again

Ingredients

Amount	Item
9 Oz	Mixed Chocolate from bars: *like dark, bittersweet, semi-sweet and milk chocolate,*
¾ Cup	Heavy Cream
¼ Cup	Unsalted Butter
2 tbsps.	Instant Espresso Granules
2 Tbsps.	Bailey's Irish Cream
8 Oz	Mixed Chocolate from bars: *like dark, bittersweet, semi-sweet and milk chocolate,*
2 Tsps.	Vegetable Oil
1 Cup	Walnut Pieces

Directions

Number	Step
1	Finely chop the first batch of chocolate bars
2	Place the chopped chocolate in a medium bowl.
3	In a heavy, medium saucepan, bring the cream and butter to a simmer
4	Pour the hot mixture over the chocolate in the bowls
5	Mix together the espresso granules and Irish Cream Liquor until dissolved
6	Let stand for 5 minutes then mix till smooth
7	Cool to room temperature and then refrigerate for 2 hours
8	Roll the mixture into 1 inch diameter balls, place on a waxed paper lined cookie sheet, refrigerate after
9	In a double boiler melt the chocolate and then add the oil.
10	Using a fork, dip the balls into the chocolate and walnuts until coated
11	Return to cookie sheet and refrigerate again

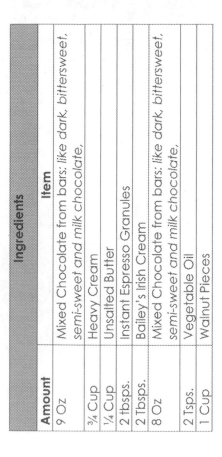

11.0 CARAMEL AND CHOCOLATE PECAN BARS

Ingredients

Amount	Item
2 Cups	All Purpose Flour
1 Cup	Firmly Packed Brown Sugar
½ Cup	Softened Margarine or Butter (1 Stick)
1 Cup +	Pecan Halves
2/3 Cup	Margarine or Butter
½ Cup	Firmly Packed Brown Sugar
1 Cup +	Semi-Sweet Chocolate Chips

Directions

Number	Step
1	Prepare crust: In large mixer bowl combine flour, brown sugar, and the 1 cup of butter
2	Beat at low speed until well mixed and particles are fine.
3	Press on bottom of 9 X 13 baking pan.
4	Sprinkle pecans over unbaked crust
5	In saucepan combine remaining butter, and brown sugar
6	Cook over medium heat until full boil.
7	Boil, stirring constantly until a candy thermometer reaches 242°F (about 2 minutes)
8	Pour over pecan and crust
9	Bake 20 +/- 2 minutes in a preheated 350°F oven or until entire caramel layer is bubbly
10	Remove from oven. Immediately sprinkle with chocolate chips, leaving some whole for effect
11	Cool completely and cut into bars

12.0 ZUCCHINI BREAD

Ingredients

Amount	Item
1 Cup	Vegetable Oil
3	Large Eggs
2 Cups	Granulated Sugar
2 Tsps.	Vanilla
2 Cups	Grated Zucchini
1 Cup	Diced Pineapple
3 Cups	All Purpose Flour
2 Tsps.	Baking Soda
1 Tsp	Salt
½ Tsp.	Baking Soda
2 Tsps.	Cinnamon
1 Tsp.	Nutmeg
1 Cup Each	Raisins and/or Walnuts (Both Optional)

Directions

Number	Step
1	Mix together oil, eggs, sugar and vanilla in a large bowl
2	Add Zucchini, Pineapple and mix well
3	Sift together Flour, baking soda, salt, baking powder, cinnamon and nutmeg
4	Add to mixture
5	Mix in raisins and nuts if desired
6	Bake in 2 greased loaf pans in preheated 350°F oven for 50 to 60 minutes

13.0 CHOCOLATE PEANUT BUTTER BARS

Ingredients

Amount	Item
2 ½ Cups	Graham Cracker Crumbs
2 ¾ Cups	Powdered Sugar
1 Cup	Peanut Butter
1 Cup	Butter, Melted
2 Cups	Semi-Sweet Chocolate Chips

Directions

Number	Step
1	In a medium bowl stir together graham cracker crumbs, powdered sugar, peanut butter and melted butter
2	Press firmly into the bottom of an ungreased 9 X 13 inch pan
3	Melt the chocolate chips and spread over the crumb crust
4	Refrigerate for 15 to 20 minutes
5	Then cut into bars before the chocolate sets completely
6	Chill until ready to serve

17

Ingredients

Amount	Item
1 Box	Yellow Pillsbury Plus Cake Mix
¼ Cup	Butter
1	Egg
3 Cups	Miniature Marshmallows
1 Large Pkg.	Reese's Peanut Butter Chips
2/3 Cup	Light Corn Syrup
2 Tsps.	Vanilla Extract
1/3 Cup	Butter
2 Cup	Rice Krispy's
2 Cups	Salted Peanuts

Directions

Number	Step
1	Mix until crumbly: cake mix, ¼ butter and 1 egg
2	Press into ungreased 9" by 13" pan.
3	Bake for 11 minutes at 350°F
4	Sprinkle 3 Cups marshmallows over this and bake for an additional 1 to 2 minutes. Then allow to cool.
5	Combine and melt Reese's peanut butter chips, corn syrup, 1/3 cup butter and vanilla extract
6	Then add Rice Krispy's and salted peanuts to this mix
7	Pour over cake and refrigerate

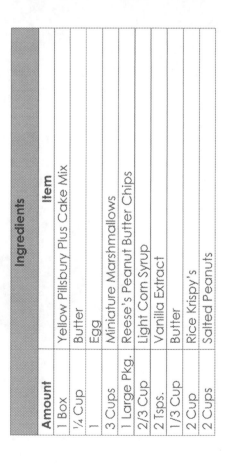

15.0 ULTIMATE TURTLE COOKIE BARS

Ingredients

Amount	Item
1 Pouch	Betty Crocker Chocolate Chip Cookie Mix
½ Cup	Butter or Margarine, Softened
1	Egg
½ Cup	Coarsely Chopped Pecans
24	Caramels, Unwrapped
1 Tbsp.	Milk
¾ Cup	Pecan halves
3 Tbsps.	Semisweet Chocolate Chips
1 Tbsp.	Shortening

Directions

Number	Step
1	In a medium bowl stir together cookie mix, butter, egg and chopped pecans until soft dough develops
2	Press evenly into an ungreased 8 inch square glass pan.
3	Bake for 30+/- 2.5 minutes, or until golden brown, in a preheated 350°F oven
4	Meanwhile, in a 1 quart saucepan, heat caramels and milk over low heat, stirring frequently
5	When melted and smooth, remove from heat
6	Carefully spread melted caramels over warm bars, sprinkle with pecan halves.
7	Cool completely on wire rack, about 1 hour
8	In small bowl, microwave chocolate chips and shortening on high for 45 +/- 15 seconds until melted
9	Drizzle over bars. Let stand until chocolate sets

Note: There is no female version, substitute any nut you like. Use a wet sharp knife to cut bars.

16.0 CONGO SQUARES

Ingredients

Amount	Item
2/3 Cup	Shortening
2 ¼ Cups	Brown Sugar, Packed
2 ¾ Cups	All Purpose Flour
2 ½ Tsps.	Baking Powder
3	Eggs
1 Tbsps.	Vanilla Extract
2 Cups	Semi-sweet Chocolate Chips

Directions

Number	Step
1	In a sauce pan melt shortening over a medium heat.
2	Stir in brown sugar. Cool slightly
3	Combine flour, baking soda and salt in a large bowl
4	Blend in shortening, brown sugar mix
5	Beat eggs and blend into mixture
S	Stir in vanilla
7	Stir in chocolate chips (and nuts, if male version is desired)
8	Spread into a greased and floured 9by 13 inch baking dish
9	Bake in a preheated oven at 350°F oven for 27.5 +/-2.5 minutes
10	Cut into squares while warm

ABOUT INGREDIENTS

Like Daddy told Momma upon the birth of a child, "See, I told you, you get out of it what you put into it".

The Cookie Lady's mother, Nellie, was typical of women who were raised during the great depression, and then married during World War II. She had two war kids and two boomer kids and she knew how to cook for a family of six using inexpensive ingredients and simple recipes.

The Cookie Lady was taught to do the same, but when it came to making cookies, only the finest, "hang the cost", ingredients are used.

From her mother-in-law, Kay, she learned the pleasure of drinking Champagne. She applied the same lesson; if one likes Champagne then "hang the cost" Champagne must be even better.

Some of the Cookie Lady's favorites to make are the chocolate truffles. However, she won't make them unless the chocolate is bought in Germany, France or Holland. Even the same brand bought in U.S.A. will never get into a truffle of hers!

Vivianism: The ingredients in a good team are very much like the makeup of a river. That is; rock, sand, detritus, debris, dead wood and enough strong willed water to carry it all.

From Mother Nellie: "Wordiness is not necessarily a sign of complex thought" Corollary: "Simple ingredients still can make a good cookie".

There are three kinds of people in any team:

- *Those with their glass half empty*
- *Those with their glass half full*
- *And those with their glass over flowing*

The cookie lady is definitely in the 3rd group.

Here you will find comments and quotes from the Engineering department who gather every other Friday to eat delicious sweets. *Anon*

"Mrs. G--you bake like nobody's business! The love you put into each batch is noticed and appreciated! Thanks for making our days here sweeter."
-Robin

"Joyce makes life at B/E fun and enjoyable. Yet most of the time she doesn't get to see how happy we are to be munching away on all of the treats she bakes for us. Every one of us looks forward to a half an hour of camaraderie with a pile of homemade cookies in front of us. It is one of the only meetings where people scramble to get there early. What a selfless act of kindness. We love the cookie lady."
-Connie

"No amount of words can truly express the tremendous teamwork displayed than that from a husband/wife team in calming the beasts in us to deal with the ferociousness of our day-to-day work."
-Harry

"Dearest Joyce (The Cookie Lady), It has been such a joy going to Bill's staff meetings knowing that your famous cookies, baked with love, care and joy, are always there in your cute little Tupperware's. Thank you so much for your many years of service! With all the sincerity that I can deliver."
-Tim

"Thank you for your kindness and for giving of yourself with each batch of cookies you bake. You are a jewel and I treasure you."

"Not what we give,
But what we share,
For the gift without the giver
Is bare." ~ James Russell Lowell
-Terri

"We sincerely appreciate the extra efforts you put in to make our meetings a pleasure with your baked goodies. Thank you very much."
-Pinky

"My little dudes love Mrs. Godecker's cookies. I usually grab a baggy for them at the meeting and we enjoy them slowly during the week while having our own mini cookie meetings. I have my 4 year old set up the table, handing out napkins, pour out milk and we try and discuss how everyone is doing. Usually our conversations are very short because they are quietly enjoying the cookies."
-Neli

"Thank you so much for all the time and effort you put into making delicious cookies for us year after year. We really enjoy them and appreciate your thoughtfulness. I hope you are doing well and wish you the best always."
-Vinita

"Dear Joyce, despite what Bill may think, we come to the meeting, but STAY for the cookies! Seriously, I can't begin to thank you enough for the kindness and generosity you have shown in baking all of those fabulous cookies for so many years. You are truly amazing and loved much!"
-Cheree

"Mrs. Godecker, you're an inspiration for putting a smile on the faces (and tummies) of a team of sweet toothed engineers. You make our Fridays really special and even make the whole work week worth it after having just one…or two…or ten bites of your delicious sweets. What makes them even more delicious is the thoughtfulness and kindness you put into every treat. It definitely makes them that much sweeter. Thank you for all your hard work and your kind gesture of sharing your amazing baked treats to the Engineering team here at B/E!"
-Janelle

"Mrs. Godecker, thank you so much for your selfless act that provides so many of us so much joy. The time and effort you put into these cookies is sensational. I have to say that the cookie meeting is a truly unique aspect that I have not experienced anywhere else. It adds to the family atmosphere of working at B/E. Words truly can't describe how lucky we are to be spoiled by you each cookie meeting. You are an amazing woman. Thank you so much for all of your efforts which make us grateful to work at B/E Aerospace."
-Gregg

"Thanks Mrs. G. for the great assortment of irresistible cookies and other treats."
-Victor

"Dear Joyce, thank-you for your making all of your wonderful cookies for our meetings over the years. Your time and effort are greatly appreciated, and without your cookies, a lot less people would show up. ☺ Thanks a bunch, you are awesome!"
-Patricia

"So Joyce puts love in 40 or more tummies about once or twice a month. It's difficult to imagine all the hours that it takes to do just that. Talk about labor of love!"
-Robert

"Sometimes I think about it, when she starts preparing and baking so many, and some of them require being cold, like the chocolate with rum, and cheesecake cups etc. However, she must like making these cookies, with all the patience, and love for Bill."
-Julian

"Thanks for all the SWEET TREATS!!!!"
-Calvin

"Thank you so much for baking cookies for our meetings on Friday. They are super delicious and I have not yet missed a meeting because of your cookies. ☺"
-*Anthony*

"Were it not for the cookies you so graciously provide us, life would be less the merrier, less the sweet sun-kissed flower it becomes because of your glorious gift. Thank you so very much."
-*Carl*

"There's only one meeting we are always early for - the cookie meeting! Thank you Mrs. Godecker for the wide variety of yumminess ☺"
-*Sarmad*

"Mrs. Godecker, thank you very much for your time to make delicious cookies for the engineering department."
-*Oender*

"Mrs. Godecker, thank you very much for taking the time to make delicious cookies for the engineering department."
-*Emad*

"The cookies are a nice mid-morning break & probably why the attendance at the meetings is generally very high."
-*Moon*

"Joyce, thank you for the amazing cookies you have baked for us. The amount of time and effort you have put in over the years is extremely selfless. I'm so glad you came up with the idea of 'Cookie meeting'! What a way to get those engineers, through their tummies ☺."
-*Sandra*

17.0 FUDGE CRINKLES WITH PEPPERMINT PATTY TOP

Ingredients

Amount	Item
1 Box	Devil's Food Cake Mix
½ Cup	Vegetable Oil
2	Large Eggs
1 Tsp.	Vanilla Extract
1 Bag	Bite Size Peppermint Patties

Directions

Number	Step
1	In a large bowl mix cake mix, oil, eggs and vanilla until dough forms
2	Drop round teaspoonful(s) onto a cookie sheet
3	Bake in preheated 350°F oven, 10 to 12 minutes
4	Lightly press one bite size peppermint patty into the center of each cookie while still warm
5	Remove to kitchen table for cooling

18.0 CINNAMON SUGAR COOKIES

Ingredients

Amount	Item
3 Tbsp.	Granulated Sugar
1 Tbsp.	Ground Cinnamon
2 ½ Cups	All Purpose Flour
½ Tsp.	Baking Soda
¼ Tsp.	Salt
1 Cup	Granulated Sugar
1 Cup	(Packed) Brown Sugar
2 Sticks	Salted Butter
2	Large Eggs
2 Tsps.	Vanilla

Directions

Number	Step
1	In a small bowl, combine sugar and cinnamon and set aside
2	In a medium bowl, combine flour, soda and salt
3	Mix well with a wire whisk and set aside
4	In a large bowl blend sugars with a mixer on medium speed
5	Add butter and mix to form a grainy paste, scraping down side of bowl
6	Mix at medium speed until light and fluffy
7	Add the flour mixture and blend at low speed
8	Shape into 1 inch balls and roll each ball in cinnamon sugar mix
9	Place on ungreased cookie sheets 2 inches apart
10	Cook in 300°F oven for 18 to 20 minutes
11	Immediately transfer to the kitchen table

19.0 ORANGE SLICE COOKIES

Ingredients

Amount	Item
½ Cup	Granulated Sugar
½ Cup	Packed Brown Sugar
½ Cup	Shortening (No Substitutes)
1	Large Egg
½ Tsp.	Vanilla Extract
1 ¼ Cup	All Purpose Flour
½ Tsp.	Baking Powder
½ Tsp.	Baking Soda
¼ Tsp.	Salt
1 Cup	Quick Cooking Oatmeal
1 Cup	Orange Slice Candy (Cut into Pieces)

Directions

Number	Step
1	In a large bowl mix sugars together
2	Then mix in shortening, egg and vanilla
3	Sift and add flour, baking powder, baking soda, and salt
4	Then mix in gently but thoroughly the oatmeal and orange slices
5	Shape into 1 inch balls and place 2 inches apart on a greased cookie sheet
6	Bake into a 375°F oven for 10 minutes or until slightly brown around the edges
7	Remove to kitchen table

20.0 LEMON SNOWFLAKES

Ingredients

Amount	Item
1 ½ Cups	All Purpose Flour
½ Tsp.	Baking Powder
½ Tsp.	Salt
½ Cup	Confectioners (powdered) Sugar
1 ¼ Cups	Granulated Sugar
4 Tsps.	Grated Lemon Zest
2 Tbsp.	Lemon Juice
4 Tbsp.	Unsalted Butter, Melted, Cooled
3 Tbsp.	Vegetable Oil
2	1 Egg whole, 1 Egg Yolk Only
1 Tsp.	Vanilla Extract

Directions

Number	Step
1	Place Confectioner's sugar in a bowl and set aside
2	Combine granulated sugar, lemon zest and whisk together
3	Sift flour, baking soda and salt and add to sugar/lemon mix. Stir until mixed
4	Cover bowl with plastic wrap and chill until dough is firm, about 1 hour
5	Roll dough into 1 inch balls, toss in confectioner's sugar
6	Place on cookie sheet about 2 inches apart
7	Bake in preheated 350°F oven for 10 to 12 minutes until they are cracked but look moist in the cracks
8	Remove to kitchen table

21.0 CHOCOLATE CHOCOLATE CHIP

Ingredients

Amount	Item
1 Cup	Butter, Softened
1 ½ Cup	Sugar, Granulated
2	Eggs
2 Tsps.	Vanilla Extract
2 Cups	Flour
2/3 Cup	Unsweetened Cocoa
¾ Tsp.	Baking Soda
¼ Tsp.	Salt
2 Cups	Semi-Sweet Chocolate Chips

Directions

Number	Step
1	In a large bowl mix together butter, sugar, eggs, and vanilla extract
2	Combine the flour, cocoa, baking soda and salt
3	Stir into butter mixture until well blended
4	Mix in the chocolate chips
5	Drop by rounded teaspoonful onto ungreased cookie sheets
6	Bake in oven preheated to 350°F for 9 +/- 1 minutes
7	Cool slightly and transfer to kitchen table

22.0 EBONY AND IVORY

Ingredients

Amount	Item
2 ¼ Cups	All Purpose Flour
½ Cup	Unsweetened Cocoa Powder
½ Tsp.	Baking Soda
¼ Tsp.	Salt
1 Cup	Packed, Dark Brown Sugar
¾ Cup	Granulated Sugar
2 Sticks	Salted Butter, Softened
3 Large	Eggs
2 Tsps.	Vanilla Extract
5 ¼ Ounces	Semisweet Chocolate Bar, Coarsely Chopped
5 ¼ Ounces	White Chocolate Bar, Coarsely Chopped

Directions

Number	Step
1	In medium bowl, combine flour, cocoa, soda and salt. Mix well, set aside
2	Blend sugars in a large bowl using an electric mixer set at medium speed
3	Add butter and mix to form a grainy paste, scraping down sides of bowl
4	Add eggs and vanilla, and beat at medium speed until smooth
5	Add mixture and chocolates and beat at medium speed. Do not over mix
6	Drop by rounded spoonful onto ungreased cookie sheet, 2 inches apart
7	Bake for 18 to 22 minutes at 300°F
8	Transfer cookies immediately to cool on kitchen table

23.0 GINGER SNAPS

Ingredients

Amount	Item
2 ½ Cups	All Purpose Flour
½ Tsp.	Baking Soda
¼ Tsp.	Salt
2 Tsps.	Ground Ginger
1 tsp.	Dice Crystalized Ginger
½ Tsp.	Allspice
½ Tsp.	Ground Black Pepper
1 ¼ Cups	Packed Dark Brown Sugar
1 ½ Sticks	Salted Butter Softened
1 Large	Egg
¼ Cup	Un-sulfurized Molasses

Directions

Number	Step
1	In a medium bowl, combine flour, soda, salt, both gingers, allspice, and pepper. Whisk well.
2	In a large bowl, mix sugar and molasses and butter with an electric mixer. Scrape down the sides of the bowl.
3	Add eggs and molasses, beat at medium speed until light and fluffy
4	Add the flour mixture and mix at low speed just until combined Do not over mix.
5	Chill the dough in a refrigerator for 1 hour.
6	Form dough into balls 1 inch in diameter
7	Place cookies on ungreased ccokie sheet 1 ½ inches apart.
8	Bake for 24 to 25 minutes
9	Trarsfer to kitchen table

24.0 KEY LIME – WHITE CHOCOLATE COOKIES

Ingredients

Amount	Item
½ Cup	Butter or Margarine, Softened
¾ Cup	Packed Brown Sugar
2 Tbsp.	Granulated Sugar
1 ½ Tsps.	Vanilla
1	Egg
2 1/3	Original Bisquick Mix
6 Drops	Green Food Coloring
1 Pkg (6 Oz)	White Baking Bar, Chocolate (Cut Into Chunks)
1 Tbsp.	Grated Lime Peel

Directions

Number	Step
1	In a large bowl, beat butter, sugars, vanilla, and egg until well mixed
2	Stir in Bisquick mix
3	Stir food coloring, white chocolate chunks and lime peel
4	Drop dough by rounded teaspoonful on ungreased cookie sheet
5	Bake 8 to 10 minutes in preheated 350°F oven or until set but not brown.
6	Cool 1 minute then remove to cooling rack

ABOUT LEADERSHIP

We should pick our leaders carefully; this is true in government as well as business

We often pick our leaders from the group of the smartest, most well-spoken Engineer, the "A player"; only to realize later that we have a lost a really good engineer and gained a bad leader.

Maybe we should pick our leaders from the middle of pack, the "B player". Pick someone who has to work hard to get noticed.

A good leader knows what Father Jeff (retired Catholic Priest) says "It is important to know who we are, who God is and do not confuse the two."

Good leaders are not worried about popularity, remember what Harry Truman asked: "How far would Moses have gone if he had taken a poll in Egypt?"

Good leaders are almost always from the glass is over flowing group. One common trait is an indelible positive spirit.

Good leaders are often thought to be good listeners. I wonder if that is true. It is said about Bill Clinton that he could walk through a large room of people, spend only a few minutes. Later, everyone would report that they had a chance to "talk to Bill" last night. Was Mr. Clinton a good listener? Is he a good leader? It may be that he saw every hand to shake as one that would also pull a lever in a voting booth and he had some quality that he imparted to others that he had been keen to hear their every word.

Leaders can't, but they lead people that can. And maybe there is a similar hidden quality there that gets people to do what needs to be done with subliminal handshakes and eye contact.

Anson said to me, "Bill, you are like most engineers, one dimensional. Leaders must be three dimensional people. Get out more; go spend time on other things, Take in the opera that is in town."

An Uncle Paul story: The Deluge

When my uncle Paul was a small boy he lived in a ramshackle wood house on a creek in the forgotten hills of Southern Indiana. This was the 1920s and 30s and in the outside world there were lights and running water and flush toilets, but not so in these beautiful, but less travelled hills. The land the family farmed was sticky clay and life was hard. In the autumn the smell of corn mash in the illegal stills would hang musky and sweet in the air.

One night a storm came up out of nowhere as Midwestern storms can do, and swept a deluge onto the farm. The creek, normally just tripping along broken slate suddenly became a torrent and threatened to take the family and the house down with it. The family escaped just in the nick of time. The house however was sent careening down the path washed out by the storm.

As the deluge subsided, the family gathered in the field in front of the now missing house. Paul's mother came running up to him, "Paul Jr. where are those new boots I just bought you?

"Ma, I put them on the front porch when I came in last night just like you told me to do", answered the young Paul.

"Well you march yourself right down the creek and get them back right now!"

Running a technical team often feels quite like that night of the deluge.

"Indecision and Delay are the parents of being late." Peter Blair

25.0 DOUBLE CHOCOLATE CHIP PEANUT BUTTER COOKIES

Ingredients

Amount	Item
6 Oz	Semi-Sweet Chocolate, Coarsely Chopped
2 Cups	All Purpose Flour
½ Tsp.	Baking Soda
¼ Tsp.	Salt
¾ Cup	Packed, Dark Brown Sugar
¾ Cup	Granulated Sugar
2 Sticks	Unsalted Butter, Softened
1 Cup	Creamy Peanut Butter
2	Large Eggs
2 Tsps.	Vanilla Extract
12 Oz	Milk Chocolate Chips (About 2 Cups)
24 to 30	Whole Shelled Peanuts

Directions

Number	Step
1	In a double boiler, melt the semisweet chocolate over hot, r ot simmering water, set aside to cool
2	In a small bowl, combine flour, baking soda and salt
3	In a medium bowl, combine the sugars, add the butter and beat until well combined
4	Add the peanut butter and beat until smooth. Blend in the eggs and vanilla extract
5	Add the flour mixture and the milk chocolate chips, beat until no streaks of flour are visible
6	Pour in the melted chocolate and mix partially with a wooden spoon until marbleized
7	Drop the dough in 3 tablespoon mounds 2 inches apart onto an ungreased cookie sheet.
8	Top each with a whole peanut. Bake in a 300°F oven for 23 minutes or until just set.
9	Allow to cool for 30 seconds then transfer to a wire rack

26.0 LEMON WHITE CHOCOLATE CHIP

Ingredients

Amount	Item
1 ½ Cups	All Purpose Flour
¾ Tsp.	Baking Soda
½ Tsp.	Salt
¾ Cup	Butter, softened
½ Cup	Packed Brown Sugar
½ Cup	Granulated Sugar
1	Large Egg
1 Tbsp.	Lemon Juice (Fresh Lemon)
2 Cups	White Chocolate Chips
1 Tsp.	Grated Lemon Peel

Directions

Number	Step
1	Combine flour, baking soda, and salt in small bowl
2	Beat butter, brown sugar and granulated sugar in large mixer bowl until creamy
3	Beat in egg and lemon juice
4	Gradually beat in flour mixture
5	Stir in chips and lemon peel (Also some nuts if male cookies desired)
6	Drop by rounded teaspoons full onto ungreased baking sheets
7	Bake for 7 to 10 minutes at 375°F
8	Cool on baking sheet for 3 minutes
9	Remove wire racks to cool completely

27.0 EGG NOG COOKIES

Ingredients

Amount	Item
2 ¼ Cups	All Purpose Flour
1 Tsp.	Baking Powder
½ Tsp.	Ground Cinnamon
½ Tsp.	Ground Nutmeg
1 ¼ Cups	Granulated Sugar
1 ½ sticks	Slated Butter, Softened
½ Cup	Eggnog
1 Tsp.	Vanilla Extract
2	Large Egg Yolks
1 Tbsp.	Ground Nutmeg

Directions

Number	Step
1	In a medium Bowl, combine flour, baking powder, cinnamon, and ½ tsp. nutmeg
2	Mix well with a wire whisk and set aside
3	In a large bowl, cream sugar and butter with an electric mixer to form a grainy paste
4	Add eggnog, vanilla and egg yolks and beat at medium speed
5	Add the flour mixture and beat at low speed until just combined. Do not over mix
6	Drop by rounded teaspoonful onto ungreased cookie sheets, one inch apart
7	Sprinkle lightly with nutmeg
8	Bake for 24 +/- 1 minute or until bottoms turn brown at 300 °F
9	Transfer to cool kitchen table immediately with a spatula

28.0 CARROT FRUIT JUMBLES

Ingredients

Amount	Item
2 ½ Cups	All Purpose Flour
1 Tsp.	Baking Soda
½ Tsp.	Baking Powder
½ Tsp.	Ground Gloves
2 Tsps.	Ground Cinnamon
¼ Tsp.	Salt
1 Cup	Quick Oats (Not Instant)
¾ Cup	Dark Brown Sugar (Packed)
¾ Cup	Granulated Sugar
2 Sticks	Salted Butter, Softened
2	Eggs
2 Tsp.	Vanilla Extract
2 Cups	Grated Carrots
½ Cup	Crushed Pineapple

Directions

Number	Step
1	In a medium bowl combine flour, soda, baking powder, cloves, cinnamon, salt and oats.
2	Mix with wire whisk and set aside
3	In a large bowl with an electric mixer, blend sugars. Add butter to form a grainy paste
4	Add eggs and vanilla and beat at medium speed
5	Add carrots, pineapple blend until combined.
6	Add flour mixture and blend at low speed until just combined, do not over mix.
7	Drop by rounded teaspoons full onto ungreased cookie sheet, 1 ½ inches apart
8	Bake in 350°F oven for 14+/- 1 minutes. Take care not to brown the cookies

29.0 CHIPPITY CHIPPERS

Ingredients

Amount	Item
2 ¾ Cups	All Purpose Flour
1 Tsp.	Baking Soda
½ Tsp.	Salt
2 Sticks	Unsalted Butter, Softened
½ Cup	Light Brown Sugar, Packed
1 Tbsp.	Honey
2	Eggs
2 Tsp.	Vanilla Extract
1 Cup	Semisweet Chocolate Chips
1 Cup	Milk Chocolate Chips
1 Cup	White Chocolate Chips
½ Cup	Peanut Butter Chips

Directions

Number	Step
1	In a medium bowl combine flour, soda and salt
2	In a large bowl cream the butter, sugars, and honey.
3	Add the eggs one at a time, beating well after each addition.
4	Beat in the vanilla and add the flour mixture
5	Add all of the chips, stir until blended, do not over mix.
6	Drop by rounded tablespoonsful 2 inches apart on ungreased cookie sheet.
7	Bake for 19+/-1 minutes in a 325°F Oven
8	Transfer to wire racks to cool.

30.0 DOUBLE RICH CHOCOLATE COOKIE

Ingredients

Amount	Item
2 ½ Cups	All Purpose Flour
½ Tsp.	Baking Soda
¼ Tsp.	Salt
½ Cup	Unsweetened Cocoa Powder
1 Cup	Dark Brown Sugar, Packed
¾ Cup	Granulated Sugar
2 Sticks	Salted Butter, Softened
3	Eggs
2 Tsp.	Vanilla Extract
2 Cups	Semisweet Chocolate Chips

Directions

Number	Step
1	In a medium bowl, combine flour, soda, salt and cocoa powder.
2	Mix well with a wire whisk.
3	In a large bowl blend sugars with a wire whisk
4	Add butter to form a grainy paste
5	Add eggs and vanilla and beat at medium speed
6	Add flour mixture and chocolate chips.
7	Blend at low speed until just combined. Do not over mix
8	Drop by rounded tablespoons onto ungreased cookie sheets 1 ½ inches apart.
9	Bake for 20 +/- 2 minutes in a 300°F oven or until cookies are light golden brown.

31.0 CHOCOLATE MINT PINWHEELS

Ingredients

Amount	Item
1 Pouch	Betty Crocker Sugar Cookie Mix
½ Cup	Butter, Softened
1	Large Egg
¼ Cup	Unsweetened Baking Cocoa
2 Tbsps.	All Purpose Flour
½ Tsp.	Mint Extract
2 to 3 Drops	Green Food Coloring

Directions

Number	Step
1	In a large bowl, stir cookie mix, butter and egg until dough forms
2	Divide dough in half. Stir Cocoa into one half.
3	Stir flour, mint extract and food color into the other half.
4	Place chocolate dough on 17 X 12 inch sheet of waxed paper.
5	Place a second sheet of waxed paper on top of the dough. Roll this into a rectangle
6	Repeat with the mint based dough. Remove the top sheet from each dough layer.
7	Using the bottom waxed paper from the mint dough invert onto the chocolate layer.
8	Using the bottom layer of waxed paper, roll up the combined dough tightly and freeze 2 hours or more
9	Unwrap dough and cut into ¼ inch slices. Place 2 inches apart on ungreased cookie sheet.
10	Bake 10 +/-1 minutes or until set. Cool 2 minutes then move to wire rack.

ABOUT THE COOKIE LADY

We were all taught as kids not to talk to strangers. The cookie lady talks to everyone, no exceptions. She is sure that even the remotest stranger wants to know how her day is going. With a glass over flowing personality, she gets a smile no matter what.

When she goes into Wal-Mart she tells the "greeter" about what she came to Wal-Mart for and why. It is not that she needs any help; it is just that she is sure that greeter wants to know.

I had a thought that when she passes from the here and now to the beyond (Hopefully, many, many years from here and now) she will meet Saint Peter much the way she does the Wal-Mart greeter; with a smile, and a few editorially words about how things are going and why she is there.

She is the daughter of a Baptist minister and it is her favorite thing to tell people. That background says a lot about her life full of basic needs. No need for fancy cars, fine clothes, or a large home. Her one swerve off the Bible Belt road is a taste for good wine. Her favorite joke goes something like:

A Presbyterian will never recognize the Pope

A Jew will never recognize Christ

And Baptist won't recognize each other going into the liquor store

32.0 MONSTER COOKIE

Ingredients

Amount	Item
1 ¼ Cup	Brown Sugar, Packed
½ Cup	Shortening
2	eggs
2 ½ Cup	Bisquick Mix, Original
1 Cup	Quick Cooking Oats
1 Cup	M&Ms
½ Cup	Raisins
½ Cup	Walnuts

Directions

Number	Step
1	In a large bowl mix brown sugar and shortening
2	Add eggs and mix thoroughly
3	Stir remaining ingredients
4	Drop by teaspoonful about 2 inches apart on ungreased cookie sheet
5	Grease the bottom of a flat bottomed glass and dip in granulated sugar
6	Flatten to about ½ inch thickness using a flat bottom glass
7	Bake 14+/1 2 minutes in oven preheated to 375°F
8	Cool 3 minutes and remove to kitchen table

33.0 CRANBERRY WHITE CHOCOLATE CHIP AND MACADAMIA NUT COOKIES

Ingredients

Amount	Item
2 Cups	All Purpose Flour
½ Tsp.	Baking Soda
½ TSP.	Salt
1 ½ Cups	Unsalted Butter, Melted and cooled slightly
1 Cup	Light Brown Sugar, Packed
½ Cup	Granulated Sugar
1	Egg plus 1 egg yolk
2 Tsps.	Vanilla Extract
1 Pkg.	White Chocolate Chips
1 Cup	Dried Cranberries, Chopped coarse
1 Cup	Macadamia Nuts, Chopped

Directions

Number	Step
1	Mix and beat in a large bowl melted butter, brown sugar and granulated sugar until smooth
2	Add egg and yolk and vanilla and mix until combined
3	Sift and add flour, baking soda and salt. Mix until just combined
4	Roll cough into 1 inch balls and space them about 2 inches apart on the cookie sheets.
5	Bake 18 =/- 2minutes until edges are set in a 325°F oven. Centers may be still soft and puffy.
6	Transfer cookies to kitchen table

34.0 LEMON CRINKLES

Ingredients

Amount	Item
½ Cup	Shortening
1 Cup	Brown Sugar Packed
1	Egg
1 Tbsp.	Grated Lemon Rind
1 ½ Cup	Flour
½ Tsp.	Soda
½ Tsp.	Cream of Tartar
¼ Tsp.	Salt
¼ Tsp.	Ginger
A/R	Granulated Sugar

Directions

Number	Step
1	Mix, shortening, brown sugar and egg thoroughly
2	Blend in lemon zest
3	Blend in dry ingredients
4	Mix all ingredients together
5	Roll into balls 1 inch in diameter
6	Dip each ball into the granulated sugar as desired
7	Bake 11 +/- 1 minutes in 350°F Oven
8	Cool on kitchen table

ABOUT FRIDAY THE 13THS; REVEALED

I met the cookie lady in August of 1979. We had both gone to work for Sundstrand Aviation in Rockford, Illinois at about the same time. We worked in a large bullpen with about 100 engineers and 5 secretaries. Joyce and I started out on opposite sides of the bullpen.

In early 1980 I was assigned to lead a technical proposal effort and Joyce was chosen to be the secretary to put it together. There were no computers or word processors back then. She was moved to a desk directly across from me. We formed a great team, I could dream, she could organize. In the parlance, they call it be whole brained when two people can fill the gaps in each other's thinking. We worked very hard to put out a very nice product.

On the 31st of March it was sent winging its way to Boeing in the hands of the marketing team. No, Virginia, Al Gore had not yet invented the internet.

On April 1st we both arrived at work with a bit of postpartum depression having seen our hard work through to a finale. At about noon I asked Joyce if she wanted to go out and celebrate for lunch. Well…the truth is we never made it to lunch and we never made it back to work either! April Fool's Day became our day.

As was the custom of those days Thursday's lunch were beer, cheeseburgers and popcorn at Opsahl's Tavern on 11th street in Rockford with a group of 15 to 20 engineers and secretaries. It happened that the 12th of June was a Thursday. Sitting in the tavern having lunch the rumor came up that the next day might be a "black Friday" with layoffs. Then someone with gallows humor pointed out that it would be a Friday the 13th as well and maybe staying home under the covers might be a good thing to do. The cookie lady looked at me, and then I look at her and from that moment on Friday the 13th became another special day. In 35 years we missed only one.

On April 1st 1982 Joyce and I left work at noon and this time we went and got our two children out from school and went down to the Justice of Peace in Winnebago County and got married. Easy thing to remember an anniversary by was having it be April Fool's Day every year.

There was one other Friday the 13th that changed our lives forever after that. In December of 1985 we stayed home on the Friday the 13th. It snowed about 6 inches during the day, but with plenty of wine and a nice fire we had no reason to worry about venturing out. At midafternoon, I got a call from my boss, Tim Morris, who said I needed to come into work for a big announcement. I told him that I could not possibly shovel the driveway in time and the effects of alcohol would make for a perilous drive.

At about 5:00 PM he called back and said "the announcement is out and there is a new engineering organizational chart with 13 names so far listed. Now there is good, bad news and just news". "Hmm.. Okay, in order please tell". He replied "Good news is you still have a job, bad news is it is not in the town you are now living, and the just news is that you have a job in San Diego if you get there next month". "Are you sure about the order of that news? Isn't San Diego in Guatemala or someplace like that? Do I need a Visa? And what about the language problem?"

35.0 I AM A GUMMY BEAR COOKIE BY TOMMY REID X

Ingredients

Amount	Item
1 Box	Rainbow Cookie Premium Sugar Cookie Mix (From Target)
½ Cup	Butter, Softened
1	Large Egg
A/R	Gummy Bears

Directions

Number	Step
1	Play the Gummy Bear Song while singing along
2	In a large bowl, combine cookie mix, softened butter and the egg. Mix until it becomes dough
3	Divide dough into 5 equal pieces and into individual, small bowls
4	Clip a small corner from each coloring packet, and then pour the following amounts onto the dough: Pink: (1/2 packet) Yellow: (1/2 packet) Blue: 7 drops Green: remainder of yellow packet plus 2 drops of blue Purple: 2 drops of blue plus 7 drops of pink
5	Using a separate spoon for each, thoroughly stir coloring into the dough until it becomes a solid color.
6	On a solid surface, gently roll each piece of colored dough into a rope about 10 inches long.
7	Place 3 ropes next to each other, then the remaining 2 on the top.
8	Twist the stacked ropes together into one large log and roll smooth.
9	Wrap in wax paper and refrigerate for 1 hour.
10	Remove wrapping. Slice the dough into ¼ inch pieces and place 2 inches apart on an ungreased cookie sheet.
11	In preheated 350°F Bake for 8-10 minutes
12	Remove from oven and place 1 Gummy Bear on top of each cookie
13	Place back in the oven for 1 minute

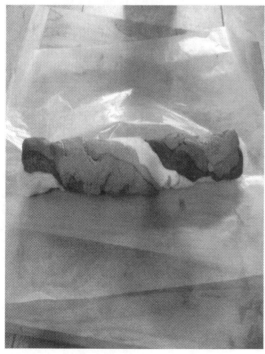 

Oh, I'm a Gummy Bear yes

Yeah, I'm a Gummy Bear yeah
Oh, I'm a Yummy, tummy, Funny, Lucky Gummy Bear.
I'm a Jelly bear, Cuz I'm a Gummy bear,
Oh I'm a movin', groovin', Jammin', Singin' Gummy Bear

Oh Yeah!

Boing day ba duty party
Boing day ba duty party
Boing day ba duty party party pop

Oh, I'm a Gummy Bear
Yes, I'm a Gummy Bear!
Oh, I'm a Yummy, Chummy, Funny, Lucky Gummy Bear.
I'm a Jelly bear, Cuz I'm a Gummy bear,
Oh I'm a movin', groovin', Jammin', Singin' Gummy Bear

Oh Yeah!

(Gummy Gummy Gummy Gummy Gummy bear)
Beba bi Duba duba yum yum
Beba bi Duba duba yum yum
Beba bi Duba duba yum yum yum
Three times you can bite me

Oh, I'm a Gummy Bear
Yes, I'm a Gummy Bear!
Oh, I'm a Yummy, Chummy, Funny, Lucky Gummy Bear.
I'm a Jelly bear, Cuz I'm a Gummy bear,
Oh I'm a movin', groovin', Jammin', Singin' Gummy Bear
Oh Yeah!

(Gummy Gummy Gummy Gummy Gummy Bear

Beba bi Duba duba yum yum
Beba bi Duba duba yum yum
Beba bi Duba duba yum yum

Three times you can bite me

Oh, I'm a Gummy Bear
Yes, I'm a Gummy Bear!
Oh, I'm a Yummy, Chummy, Funny, Lucky Gummy Bear.
I'm a Jelly bear, Cuz I'm a Gummy bear,
Oh I'm a movin', groovin', Jammin', Singin' Gummy Bear

Oh Yeah!

Haha Duba duba yum yum
Haha Duba duba yum yum
Haha Duba duba yum yum
Three times you can bite me

"I like working with engineers, not many non-technical people can say that", the Cookie Lady

Some people say thank God its Friday, the cookie lady says "Thank God it's a cookie week!"

Printed in the United States
By Bookmasters